DATE DUE

MAR 5 '92		
MAY 6 '92		
NOV 6 '92		
MAR 10 '93		
MAY 12 '93		

Environmental

AMERICA

Environmental
AMERICA

The South Central States

———————

by
D.J. Herda

The Millbrook Press
Brookfield, CT
The American Scene

Cover photographs (clockwise from top) courtesy of Texas Tourist Agency;
D. J. Herda (2); Wisconsin Division of Tourism

Inside photographs courtesy of U.S. Environmental Protection Agency: 17, 22, 24, 34,
37, 38; Wisconsin Department of Natural Resources: 13, 19, 32, 50; Louisiana State
Tourism Department: 2, 6; Texas Tourist Agency: 14, 28-29; Mammal Slide Library,
P. V. August: 42; TTDA, Michael Murphy: 45; D. J. Herda: 7, 10

Designed by Moonlit Ink, Madison, WI 53705
Illustrations by Renee Graef

Cataloging-in-Publication Data

Herda, D. J.
Environmental America: The South Central States.
Brookfield, CT, The. Millbrook Press. 1991.
64 p.; col. ill.; (The American Scene)
Includes bibliographical references and index.
Summary: The impact of humankind and society on the environment,
with special emphasis on the South Central region
ISBN 1-878841-09-2   639.9/HER

1. Gulf states—environmental impacts—juvenile literature.
2. Conservation of natural resources. 3. Pollution.
[1. Environmental America: The South Central States] I. Title. II. Series.

CONTENTS

Introduction
7

The Land We Walk
11

The Air We Breathe
25

The Water We Drink
35

A Time for Action
43

What We Can Do
51

For More Information
54

Notes
57

Glossary
58

Bibliography
61

Index
63

INTRODUCTION

The South Central United States ranges from the Gulf states of Alabama, Mississippi, Louisiana, and Texas and the flatlands of Oklahoma and Kansas to the rolling hills of Missouri, Arkansas, Kentucky, and Tennessee. The region varies widely in both climate and natural environment. Not surprisingly, it has also had a rich, diverse history.

The state of Tennessee was originally claimed as a colony by Virginia and, later, North Carolina. It wasn't until Daniel Boone traveled through the region in the 1760s, though, that the eastern United States learned of the area's vast diversity of terrain and wildlife.

Missouri, to the north and west of Tennessee, was part of the French-held Louisiana Territory into the early 1800s. It built its reputation around the founding of St. Louis in 1765 where the mighty Missouri and Mississippi rivers meet. Along the shores of these two great waterways lay wetlands teeming with life.

For years, Texas was an important part of Spain's holdings in North America. It was ceded to Mexico when that country won its independence from Spain. After years of clashes between the Mexican and Anglo cultures living in the region, Texas broke away from Mexico. For the next decade, it survived as an independent country before becoming a state in 1845.

THE LOUISIANA PURCHASE

Throughout the South Central region, the greatest environmental diversity is found in the state of Louisiana, a low-lying area bordering the Mississippi River on the west and the Gulf of Mexico on the south. An area rich in wetlands, coastal estuaries, and natural resources, Louisiana was once part of the Spanish-held region that extended from the Mississippi River west to Colorado and north to present-day Canada.

(opposite page)
Steamboats have been part of the heritage of the Mississippi River for nearly 200 years.

On hearing the news that Spain had secretly ceded Louisiana to France in order to satisfy the ambitious French emperor Napoleon, an anxious President Jefferson sent a committee to France to purchase New Orleans and western Florida for $2 million. The French were in desperate need of money to fund their involvement in Europe's Napoleonic Wars. They countered the U.S. proposal by offering to sell the entire Louisiana Territory for $15 million. The area was officially ceded to the United States in 1803, doubling the country's size and bringing new and valuable environmental resources to a budding young nation.

A WIDE RANGE OF BIOMES

Today, the South Central region of the United States includes several distinct environments, called biomes. These range from the pine forests in the eastern part of the region (coniferous biomes) and the coastal sands of the Gulf area (coastal wetland biomes) to the upland prairies of Kansas and Missouri (grassland biomes). All these biomes play host to numerous species of wildlife: raccoons and mockingbirds; armadillos and eagles; deer and flycatchers; bluebirds and largemouth bass; crawfish and alligators; wild turkey and cardinals.

Poisonous insects and lizards inhabit the South Central region, too. Venomous snakes slither through the bayous of the coastal wetlands and across the burning sands of Texas and Oklahoma. Every species has a place in the ecological scheme of things. Every creature plays its part—from animals and plants down to fungi and single-celled bacteria.

(opposite page)
The simple spider is actually a complex cog in nature's chain of life.

But the South Central United States is quite different today from what it was 200, 100, or even 50 years ago. Its face has been changed by the woodsman's ax and saw. Its body has been changed, too. Today, the land is poisoned with toxic substances where yesterday there was life. The air is clouded with dust and pollutants. The waters run foul, courtesy of an indifferent industrial complex

In fewer than 250 years, the South Central United States has changed from a thriving, diverse, healthy ecosystem to something much more delicate and fragile. One of the world's most ecologically exciting regions totters on the brink of disaster.

8

THE LAND
WE WALK

Most of the wildlife of the South Central states lives and thrives in the wilderness-rich areas of the wetlands and coastal regions. From these areas, the first single-celled organisms—followed by more complex plants and finally animals—emerged from ancient rivers, estuaries, and swamps to begin life on land. The right nutrients, moisture, and light allowed them to grow and multiply until the lands were teeming with life.

Ancient rock fossils show that much of what is now the South Central region was once covered by swamps and marshes. During this time, wildlife experienced remarkable periods of growth. The largest land animals that ever lived, the sauropod dinosaurs, grew to nearly 90 feet in length and weighed more than 75 tons. Most of their bulk came from food skimmed from the rich wetlands. The dinosaurs' modern-day reptilian contemporaries, alligators and crocodiles, still reach their greatest size in wetlands.

(opposite page)
Wetlands are becoming endangered throughout the South Central region as runoff and sediment gradually fill them in.

Today's wetlands play host to plants such as the bald cypress and provide an important link between land and water. They offer perfect growing conditions for modern plant species such as cattails, sedges, rushes, cordgrass, pickleweeds, willows, and mangroves. In addition, storks, small fish, snakes, and numerous crustaceans thrive in wetlands.

OUR DISAPPEARING WETLANDS

But many wetlands in the South Central states disappeared soon after the first colonists arrived from Europe. The colonists brought with them a built-in prejudice against wetlands, for in

Europe they were regarded as breeding grounds for insects and disease.

Although some large wetland areas still existed along the Atlantic coast by the early 1900s, years of filling in the swamps and dredging for recreational and real estate developments destroyed a large number of them. A few large tracts still remain along the Gulf coasts of Texas and Louisiana, but most have long since disappeared. With them have gone the plants, fish, birds, and other animals that once lived there.

THE FOOD CHAIN

Green plants are the most basic component in nature's food chain. As the plants grow, they provide food for a large number of herbivores, or plant-eating animals. The herbivores subsequently are eaten by carnivores, or meat-eating animals. Smaller carnivores are eaten by larger ones. As the largest animals die, their bodies decompose, breaking down into minerals and other basic elements that eventually return to nourish the soil for new plants.

In the South Central states, the food chain often begins with cordgrass sprouting in the bayous, or marshlands, of southern Louisiana. Small crayfish feed on tender green sprouts. Fingerling bass feed on the crayfish. Wading birds feed on the bass. Alligators feed on the wading birds. The chain is complete when the alligators die and their bodies decompose back into the minerals and other nutrients from which the cordgrass originally sprouted. Eventually, a new chain is born.

(opposite page)
Throughout the South Central region, wading birds play an important role in maintaining nature's delicately balanced food chain.

But this complex chain may be easily broken. When developers cut down the cordgrass and drain the bayou to build a new housing development, the crayfish disappear. Without crayfish, fingerling bass in nearby ponds decrease in number. Without fingerlings, the wading birds slowly diminish in population. The alligators soon move out in search of food. Eventually, little wildlife is left.

Less wildlife also means fewer carcasses. This, in turn, means less decomposition and fewer nutrients returning to the soil. Without nutrients, the remaining cordgrass eventually thins out, then disappears altogether. With it goes the rest of the food chain.

THE DUST BOWL

Around the turn of the century, thousands of farmers and ranchers were living in the upper South Central states. The rich, tallgrass prairies provided excellent grazing for cattle and high-yielding fields for sprawling crops of wheat.

But soon the livestock overgrazed much of the land. Native grasses fell to farmers' plows. Rich fields of green slowly turned into barren deserts of brown. Pastures that had once supported a hundred steers soon could support only a small number. Land that once produced 50 bushels of wheat an acre soon was yielding 40, 30, and 25.

The winds that pounded the open range picked up valuable topsoil and scattered it across the countryside. Sudden rains created flash floods that sent whatever topsoil was left rushing toward the sea. Thick mats of weeds quickly sprouted over huge areas.

Finally, the summer droughts came. High temperatures were accompanied by month after month of little or no rain. From the rangelands of the agricultural Southwest through the prairie lands of the fertile Midwest, huge crops of wheat and other grains failed.[1] Poor farming practices resulted in massive windswept clouds of dust so thick, one farmer remarked that it was like living in a darkened closet 24 hours a day. Up to 25,000 acres of the world's most fertile topsoil literally vanished in the wind, picked up and scattered as far as Maryland, Virginia, and North Carolina—more than a thousand miles away! Animals died from thirst and starvation. People perished, too—those who didn't pack up and move away.

That was the beginning of the Dust Bowl—the South Central states' worst agricultural disaster. Farmers and ranchers by the thousands in Kansas, Missouri, Oklahoma, Texas, and Arkansas followed old pioneer trails west to California, hoping for better opportunities. Some found them; others failed.

In less than half a century, humanity in its ignorance had turned lush stands of grass into barren wastelands. Where once endless fields of wheat, oats, and rye rustled lightly in the wind, now sagebrush, tumbleweed, and other useless shrubs dotted the countryside.

*(opposite page)
Cattle have been an economic necessity– and an ecological nightmare– for nearly a century.*

15

The native wildlife population suffered, too. As the lush grasslands disappeared, so did thousands of species of insects, birds, reptiles, and mammals that had made them their home. People had learned the hard way that abusing the land had its price. As the country plummeted deeper and deeper into an economic depression, that price turned out to be very high, indeed.

NEW THREATS FOR AGRICULTURAL LANDS

Farmers have been irrigating their fields for more than a thousand years. By 1900, approximately 99 million acres of land worldwide were regularly being irrigated—flooded with water diverted from rivers and streams to farmers' fields—for agricultural purposes. By 1950, that total had nearly doubled. Since then, the number of acres under irrigation has exploded, nearly tripling between 1950 and 1985 and boosting worldwide food production. A vast irrigation system in Asia, for example, has enabled farmers there to feed nearly half the world's population.

But when water is diverted from rivers, lakes, streams, and underground aquifers to irrigate nearby farmlands, salt rises from deep within the soil to the surface. There it gradually increases the salinity of the topsoil and reduces its fertility. This process, called salinization, has created a serious problem in America's South Central states, where increased irrigation has resulted in highly saline soils, especially in the arid lands of Oklahoma, Texas, and southern Missouri.

Irrigation is also depleting underground aquifers, from which agricultural and urban fresh water comes. The water level of the Ogallala, which supplies six states with water for irrigation, is rapidly falling. The problem is most severe in the Sunbelt states, especially in Texas, where booming human populations are diverting underground water supplies from farmers' fields.

As a result, farmers are slowly turning away from the practice of irrigating their lands. But the increase in salinity and decrease in groundwater levels may never allow the land to return to its original state.

World Land Area Suitable for Agriculture

No Limitations	11%
Too Wet	10%
Too Shallow	22%
Chemical Problems	23%
Too Dry	28%
Unaccounted	6%

Satellite topographical studies show that, of all the world's land, very little is actually suitable for agricultural use.

Source: Essam, El-Hinnawi and Mansur, Hashmi, *The State of the Environment* (London: Butterworths, 1987), p. 36

AGRICULTURAL WASTES

Another problem facing the region's agricultural industry is the increased use of chemical pesticides on croplands. The chemical pesticide endrin is 300 times more toxic than DDT for some wildlife species. It's also a proven carcinogen, or cancer-causing agent. Exposure to it can lead to severe nausea, convulsions, birth defects, brain damage, and nervous system disorders. A quarter of an ounce can kill in less than an hour.

Soil erosion is one of the most serious problems facing the agricultural South.

Yet endrin has been widely used throughout the South Central states for years. In the early 1960s, millions of fish in the Mississippi River died because of endrin discharges from a Velsicol Chemical Corporation plant producing the pesticide in Memphis, Tennessee. The Environmental Protection Agency

17

(EPA) subsequently banned some uses of endrin, particularly on tobacco and nursery plants, but failed to ban the pesticide altogether. In the 1970s, endrin was sprayed on 5.5 million acres of farmland in Kansas and Oklahoma, causing the widespread death of both livestock and wildlife.

"The ramifications of [endrin] spraying are mind-boggling," says Dr. John Drynan, Montana health commissioner. "One of the things I'm concerned about is the leaching process. If we wait a year or two, will endrin end up in our groundwater supplies and well water?"

Dr. Drynan's fears are well founded. Tests have shown that endrin remains a hazard in the environment for a minimum of 12 to 14 years. Worse, endrin passes up the food chain to the fatty tissues of birds, animals, and, ultimately, people.

ALTERNATIVES TO PESTICIDES

Environmentalists and many home gardeners have known for decades that food crops can be grown without the use of chemical fertilizers and pesticides. By alternating different plants to discourage insect infestations and using harmless natural substances such as crushed marigold petals and ground black pepper, insect damage can be held to a minimum. But for years farmers have downplayed such remedies on a large scale. New research and field testing, though, have recently shown that organic techniques can be used successfully on a larger scale.

The U.S. Department of Agriculture has recently overseen several integrated pest management (IPM) programs. These rely on biological controls such as natural predators of pests and the creation of pest-resistant plants. The results prove that IPM is economically feasible for over 40 different crops. As a bonus, farmers using IPM substantially reduced the amount of toxic chemicals in their fields.[2]

THE DANGERS OF LOGGING

But agriculture isn't the only threat to the region's environment. Throughout the South Central United States, massive logging operations have virtually destroyed all the old-growth forests and pushed numerous animal species to the edge of extinction. Both the ivory-billed and red-cockaded woodpeckers depend on old-growth pines—trees a minimum of 80 years old—for survival. Since the destruction of these forests, both types of woodpeckers have dropped in numbers to the point where they're now endangered species.[3] Many believe the ivory-billed woodpecker may already be extinct.

Yet the logging continues.

Texas' Big Thicket, a combination of eight biological communities ranging from sandy arid lands to acidic bogs, is home to more than 1,000 species. "What we have in the Big Thicket National Preserve aren't unusual species so much as unusual combinations of species," according to ranger Dave

Poor logging practices and forest mismanagement have led to disastrous losses of virgin timber and natural habitat.

Baker. Yucca and dogwood, roadrunners and egrets, prickly pear cactus and bald cypress, and otters and armadillos all live together in what the United Nations designated as a "Man and Biosphere Reserve" in 1981. In some places, according to residents, the vegetation is so thick that snakes have to backtrack to get out.

But Big Thicket, which once covered eastern Texas from the Louisiana border to as far west as Houston, is hurting. Only 8 percent of the original area remains intact. As a result, the bears, mountain lions, and ivory-billed woodpeckers are gone. Huge tracts of native trees have been logged. In their place now stand commercial pine plantations. Big Thicket, according to one local environmentalist, was "sold out."

Nearly 85,000 acres were originally protected by legislation passed in 1974. However, conservationists were disappointed that some key lands called the "Lost Heart" had been excluded. These unprotected lands included a winding stream with sandy banks and a natural corridor for wildlife called Big Sandy.

The Lost Heart was excluded from protection, according to the Sierra Club's Brand Mannchen, because of certain groups that pressured U.S. Congressman Charles Wilson, who "made it very plain that if a bill were to be passed [protecting Big Thicket], these areas had to be left out." But Wilson, who once managed a timber company lumberyard, surprised environmentalists when he recently agreed to sponsor a bill restoring 14,000 acres of missing lands, including Big Sandy, to the preserve.

Not surprisingly, the timber industry opposes the bill. So do local residents, who fear losing their property rights to the federal government. "The locals are being surrounded by clear-cuts [massive logging operations], but they don't want the federal [government's] presence," says Mannchen.

The locals, led by Hector Garcia, president of the Angelina County branch of the Texas Farm Bureau, admit they "oppose the taking of private property."

As part of a compromise, Wilson has revised his bill to protect homeowners. But the Farm Bureau still opposes the bill, partly because ranchers would no longer be allowed to run cattle in Big Thicket.

After Wilson's bill passed the House of Representatives, fellow Texan Lloyd Bentsen agreed to sponsor legislation in the Senate. Meanwhile, the battle lines remain as local ranchers and logging companies prepare to slug it out with environmentalists. The fate of thousands of acres of the Lost Heart hangs in the balance.[4]

THE TOXIC-WASTE PROBLEM

Loss of habitat to logging and other commercial development is a serious problem throughout the South Central states. However, another problem dwarfs it by comparison. Often called by environmentalists the most frightening dilemma facing humanity today, toxic wastes threaten our very survival on Earth.

Toxic wastes—poisonous waste products generated by industry and agriculture—include such hazardous substances as carcinogenic chemical compounds, pesticides, fertilizers, heavy metals, and wastes from nuclear power and weapons plants. Nearly 70 percent of all toxic wastes produced in the United States come from the chemical and petrochemical, or fossil-fuel refinery, industries. Nearly one fifth of the nation's petrochemical production is concentrated along an 85-mile stretch on the Mississippi River winding south from Baton Rouge to New Orleans, Louisiana. This single stretch absorbs more toxins, including such dangerous substances as the proven carcinogen polyvinyl chloride (PVC), than do most entire states.

About two thirds of all toxic wastes are disposed of in landfills or in wells, pits, or ponds. But all these sites are subject to leaking, which can contaminate groundwater. Another one fifth of the nation's hazardous waste is dumped into sewers or directly into streams and rivers. Only about 11 percent is recycled or processed to eliminate or reduce toxicity.

So far, the EPA has identified at least 15,000 uncontrolled landfills containing toxic waste throughout the United States. Another 80,000 toxin-contaminated surface lagoons are slowly seeping their poisonous pollutants into the environment. The problem is so widespread that eight out of ten Americans now live near a toxic-waste site, according to the Council on

Toxic Substances Discharged by U.S. Industry, 1987

Destination	Millions of Pounds
Air	2700
Lakes, Rivers and Streams	550
Landfills and Earthen Pits	3900
Treatment and Disposal Facilities	3300
Total	10450

Source: Environmental Protection Agency, reported in *The Washington Post*, April 13, 1989, p. A33

Economic Priorities. Nearly half of all U.S. residents live in counties containing at least one site designated by the EPA as among the most dangerous in the country.[5] From 1982 to 1988, 11,048 toxic spills caused a total of 309 deaths and 11,341 injuries nationwide.

One of the worst producers of toxic wastes, according to a 1983 study by the Department of Commerce and Congressional Budget Office, is the state of Louisiana. It ranked number one at 3.1 metric tons of waste per capita. Tennessee ranked number three at 2.6 metric tons. Texas ranked number four at 2.2 metric tons. In fact, nine out of ten of the South Central states ranked among the top 25 toxic-waste producers in the nation. Five out of ten placed in the top ten![6]

All tolled, Texas tops the region's list for the greatest number of hazardous-waste sites with 28, according to the EPA. Missouri is close behind with 21. Tennessee follows with 17, while Louisiana has 11.

THE HAZARDS OF HAZARDOUS WASTE

Hazardous-waste disposal can cause serious problems for the environment. One of the nation's most notorious mishaps occurred in Times Beach, Missouri, when a waste-oil dealer was asked by a chemical manufacturer to dispose of a small quantity of a highly toxic chemical. The dealer unwittingly created a sludge by mixing the chemical with waste oil and spraying the oil mix on the town's streets to help settle the summer dust. After more than a decade of spraying, a flood in 1982 brought the chemical contamination to the attention of officials, who diagnosed the sludge as containing dioxin, one of the most deadly synthetic substances known.

In 1983, as dioxin levels in the town rose to 300 times higher than those considered safe for humans, the federal government paid all 2,400 Times Beach residents to evacuate their homes. It also began the $64 million process of removing the toxin. As costly as the cleanup was, its expense was minimal compared with the long-term health care costs for those exposed to the toxin.[7]

(opposite page)
The safe disposal of hazardous waste is one of the most serious problems currently facing the South Central states.

23

THE AIR
WE BREATHE

Many people think of the skies over the South Central United States as sunny and blue all year long. And sometimes they are—especially in the coastal region stretching along the Gulf from eastern Alabama to western Texas.

But there's something else in the South Central region's skies, too. It's pollution—some of which comes from nature itself!

POLLUTION FROM NATURAL—
AND UNNATURAL—SOURCES

Each and every day, such naturally occurring pollutants as methane, ozone, sulfur dioxide, nitrogen oxides, carbon monoxide, hydrocarbons, lead, and particulates enter the atmosphere. They come from dozens of natural sources such as forest fires, volcanic eruptions, and the decaying of dead plants and animals.

But nature the polluter is also nature the cleanser. Over millions of years of evolution, the environment has developed different ways to neutralize the pollutants from natural causes. What it hasn't learned to do is neutralize anthropogenic pollutants—those caused by humans.

Today, the skies over the South Central states are cleaner than they were just 20 years ago. Concentrations of harmful lead have dropped nearly 90 percent, mostly due to strictly enforced auto-pollution emission standards and a shift to unleaded motor fuel. Carbon monoxide from motor vehicle exhausts has likewise dropped.

Yet, worldwide, human activities resulted in the release in 1980 of about 110 million tons of sulfur oxides. These were

(opposite page)
Although the South Central states have dramatically reduced some forms of air pollution, the hazardous pollutants still filling the skies far exceed levels considered safe for the environment.

joined by 69 million tons of nitrogen oxides, 193 million tons of carbon monoxide, 57 million tons of hydrocarbons, and 59 million tons of particulates. That's a total of 488 million tons—nearly 1 trillion pounds!—of only the world's five most common air pollutants.[1] An EPA study in 1987 revealed some 308 different toxic chemicals in America's air.

Nearly half of the world's air pollutants originates in the 24 industrial nations of the Organization for Economic Cooperation and Development (OECD). The rest are emitted by the world's remaining 148 nations and 33 territories combined.

Air pollution is obviously a by-product of industrialization. Along with increased numbers of furnaces, boilers, generating plants, and motor vehicles comes increased pollution.

URBAN AIR POLLUTION

The damage to the environment caused by air pollution has been documented for decades. The hazards to humans have only recently been studied, and the full extent of those hazards is still greatly unknown. But what is known is frightening.

After just one day of high air pollution concentrations, many people experience watery eyes, shortness of breath, mild chest pains, or burning in the throat or lungs. Longer exposures may lead to seizures, disorders of the nervous system, damage to the heart and lung tissues, and even death.

The EPA has identified and defined six major air pollutants as common to major metropolitan areas.

- *Total suspended particulates (TSP)*—The name given to any particle or group of particles such as pollen, soot, asbestos, sand, and dust borne by the wind. The level of particulates in the air generally increases from west to east, since that's usually the prevailing wind direction. Particulates in South Central cities are often found in greatest concentrations in and around Dallas, Houston, Birmingham, Kansas City, Knoxville, Baton Rouge, St. Louis, and Oklahoma City. The EPA estimates that more than 6 million tons of particulates were released in the United States in 1987.

- *Sulfur dioxide*—An arid, corrosive gas produced by burning high-sulfur coal. Sulfur dioxide comes from coal-burning power plants in Illinois, Indiana, Ohio, Kentucky, West Virginia, and Pennsylvania.

- *Carbon monoxide*—When inhaled in great enough concentrations, carbon monoxide enters the bloodstream and prevents the body from absorbing oxygen. This eventually results in death. In lesser concentrations, it causes impaired vision, poor coordination, and a heart condition known as angina. Carbon monoxide is created by the incomplete combustion of fossil fuels. Since nearly 75 percent of the carbon monoxide in the air comes from automobiles, the greatest concentrations of this pollutant in the South Central region are found in major metropolitan areas such as Dallas/Ft. Worth, Houston, Kansas City, and St. Louis. Among cities ranked by the amount of carbon monoxide in their air, El Paso, Texas, and Fairbanks, Arkansas, place in the top ten.

- *Photochemical oxidants, or smog*—A group of chemicals that combine in the presence of strong sunlight to create such harmful compounds as nitrous oxides, hydrocarbons, and ozone. These oxidants are formed by combining sunshine, which is plentiful throughout the South Central region, with automobile exhaust, which is increasing at an alarming rate. Smog is the fastest growing and most difficult to control of all urban air pollutants.

- *Lead*—A poisonous element that usually occurs as a heavy metal but may also appear in air, water, and even animal tissue. Lead in living tissue interferes with various biochemical reactions, leading to mental retardation and numerous physical ailments. Since the mandatory use of unleaded gasoline, the major source of airborne lead has been greatly reduced.[2]

Although most cities in the South Central United States have relatively low levels of another major air pollutant—ozone—Houston ranks second behind Los Angeles as the worst ozone polluter in the nation.

CHEMICAL POLLUTANTS

Another villain hard at work throughout the South Central region poisons the air around the clock. Each year, billions of

The Dallas skyline,
once one of the cleanest
in the nation, today is
fouled by smog and
other urban pollutants.

pounds of toxic chemicals belch out of smokestacks and into the atmosphere. Worst of all, most are perfectly legal!

Various controls on the disposal of toxic wastes in landfills and waterways were established following worldwide attention to disasters such as Times Beach, Missouri, in the 1970s and Love Canal (in upstate New York) in 1978. But the air has received far too little protection. As a result, it's fouled by hundreds of chemicals. These include dozens that are known to cause birth defects, cancer, genetic mutations, and chronic illness in human beings.

A 1985 study by the EPA showed that 17 toxic air pollutants cause an estimated 2,000 cancer cases a year nationwide. Among the nation's worst polluters is a group of chemical plants along the Mississippi River north of New Orleans.

In 1987, 38 major chemical companies in an area known as "Cancer Alley" discharged nearly 400 million pounds of toxins into the surrounding environment. Downriver from the plants, cancer rates in New Orleans are among the highest in the nation. In seven out of ten Louisiana parishes, or counties, along "Cancer Alley," cancer rates are substantially higher than the national average. Cancer rates among women in Louisiana's St. Charles parish are rising 18 times faster than for American women as a whole.[3]

Many of the chemical companies in "Cancer Alley" argue that there's no relationship between their plants' emissions and the high cancer rates. But their victims don't agree, and a growing number of physicians, public health officials, environmentalists, and medical researchers feel likewise.

Ironically, the federal government and various state governments have set limits on dumping hazardous chemicals in water and in landfills. But the toxins regularly emitted into the air eventually settle to Earth to pollute our land and water—often many miles from their source.

Of the 20 companies with the highest toxic air emissions reported to the EPA by the Natural Resources Defense Council in 1987, ten are located in the South Central region—one each in Alabama, Arkansas, and Mississippi; two each in Tennessee and Texas; and three in Louisiana. Together, these 10 plants accounted for more than 215 million pounds of toxic chemical emissions released into the atmosphere.[4]

Although toxic pollutants are a serious problem throughout the South Central United States, another problem is equally serious. It's called the greenhouse effect.

THE GREENHOUSE EFFECT

Numerous gases collecting in the Earth's atmosphere act as a shield to trap radiant heat from the sun and prevent it from escaping back into space. The resulting "greenhouse effect" is causing atmospheric temperatures to rise around the world.

The four most common greenhouse gases are methane, chlorofluorocarbons (CFCs), nitrogen oxides, and carbon dioxide. As these gases accumulate, heat continues to build up. Scientists estimate that the Earth's average temperature has already risen 1° F during the last 100 years and that it could increase by as much as 2 to 8° in the future. An 8° average temperature increase would make the Earth warmer than it's been in the last 2 million years!

Although a few degrees may not seem like a great amount, increases of only 3 to 4° could change the world's climate enough to reduce global rainfall, trigger worldwide droughts, spark global famine, and cause the world's ice caps to melt faster than usual. That could result in rising sea levels and flooding that would be particularly destructive to the South Central region's low-lying coastal areas. Hundreds of plant and animal species could disappear in a matter of a few decades.[5]

Interestingly, although the Earth has warmed 1° F worldwide during the last century, the United States hasn't. In fact, evidence points to some parts of the Northern Hemisphere that are actually experiencing cooler winters. The reason, according to scientists, is that increasing greenhouse gases may also increase cloud cover in some regions. The clouds block more incoming solar radiation than the outgoing radiation they trap, causing regional cooling.

As greenhouse gases accumulate and the Earth's average temperature rises, local climates may become even more variable—warmer and drier in some parts of the country and cooler and wetter in others. Some regions could even experience both hotter summers *and* colder winters.[6]

CARBON DIOXIDE'S ROLE
IN GLOBAL WARMING

Although reforestation helps to reduce the number of greenhouse gases in the air, the South Central region needs a comprehensive forest management program geared to the protection of the area's fragile environment.

Of all the greenhouse gases, carbon dioxide is the most important. It accounts for nearly half of all greenhouse effects. Before the Industrial Revolution, the concentration of carbon dioxide in the Earth's atmosphere was between 275 and 285 parts per million (ppm). During the last 30 years, carbon dioxide from burning fossil fuels—coal, oil, and natural gas—has risen by 25 percent and continues to increase.[7] At that rate, scientists predict that the overall warming of the Earth in the next century will be 10 to 40 times greater than during the global warming following the last great Ice Age some 11,000 years ago.

As a result, the average number of 100° days in Memphis could rise by the year 2050 from 4 to 42 and in Dallas from 19 to 78.[8] These increases could severely affect wildlife in the South Central states. Since trees are especially sensitive to climate variations, entire forests would be threatened. Trees would also become more susceptible to disease, insects, and other natural stresses.[9] Many animals, unable to migrate to cooler climates as quickly as in the past because of such "civilization locks" as roads, farms, towns, and cities, would perish. Even food crops would suffer. A 3° increase in temperature combined with a 10 percent decrease in precipitation could reduce U. S. corn production by one fifth.[10]

EPA PLAN

In an effort to halt the greenhouse effect, the EPA has proposed a multistep plan aimed at reducing the amount of greenhouse gases in the environment:

1. Raise the prices of the fossil fuels that generate greenhouse gases, thus discouraging their use.
2. Increase the use of alternative energy sources such as solar and nuclear power that don't produce greenhouse gases.
3. Grow new forests around the planet. Trees consume carbon dioxide and produce oxygen; the more trees, the less carbon dioxide in the atmosphere.
4. Stop the use of chlorofluorocarbons, chemicals once commonly used as propellants in aerosol cans.
5. Capture and neutralize methane gas escaping from landfills.
6. Change techniques for raising both rice and cattle, two major producers of methane.[11]

Even if such a plan were implemented on a worldwide basis by the year 1992, though, scientists estimate that the rate of gas buildup in the atmosphere wouldn't end until sometime in the twenty-second century. This would result in an unavoidable warming of from 1 to 2° F.

U.S. Sources of Carbon Dioxide Emissions

Electric Utilities	33%
Transportation	31%
Industry	24%
Buildings	12%

Source: MacKenzie, *Breathing Easier* p.10

CHAPTER THREE

THE WATER WE DRINK

Three quarters of the Earth is composed of water that has remained relatively pure for millions of years. But today, countless lakes, rivers, ponds, and streams of the South Central states are threatened by chemical runoff, motorboat pollutants, solid waste from urban developments, toxic waste from landfills, oil spills from ships at sea, and countless other sources of pollution. Even the Gulf of Mexico is becoming a giant cesspool for the nation's garbage and hazardous wastes.

Still the pollution continues. And nowhere is it of greater concern to the South Central states than it is in the coastal wetlands.

LOUISIANA'S WETLANDS

Once scattered across 215 million acres of what is now the continental United States, wetlands today occupy an estimated 99 million acres—less than 50 percent of their original size. Yet wetlands play a critical role in replenishing groundwater and in acting as a natural water purifier. They also help control flooding and prevent soil erosion.[1]

Wetland plants absorb excess nutrients and help to prevent pesticides, heavy metals, and other toxins from moving up the food chain. Wetlands also provide a home for many unique species of wildlife and a breeding ground for numerous fish and waterfowl.

But the United States is losing its wetlands to urban and agricultural development at an estimated rate of 450,000 acres a year.[2] In Louisiana alone, the loss of wetlands is estimated at 50 to 60 square miles a year and is increasing. These losses

(opposite page)
Pure water is the base for all life on Earth; yet it's disappearing at a staggering rate.

account for nearly 80 percent of all coastal wetlands lost each year in the continental United States.

For thousands of years, the area now known as Louisiana lost countless acres of wetlands through natural causes. These losses were offset by new wetlands created from silt and sediment deposited by rivers flowing into the Gulf of Mexico. Today, however, wetland losses are outstripping any buildup of new land. One of the biggest reasons involves one of the world's mightiest rivers—the Mississippi—or, rather, people's manipulation of the river.[3]

Through the construction of levees along the main channel of the river, new areas of open water are constantly being formed. The levees funnel sediment down artificial channels into the Gulf of Mexico, preventing it from being deposited in coastal marshlands. The result is that new wetlands are no longer being created to take the place of those lost from natural and artificial causes. Jetties, built at the mouth of the Mississippi for the purpose of preventing sediment buildup, help funnel the sediment out past the continental shelf.[4]

The loss of Louisiana's wetlands is a tragedy to the environment. Without vast stretches of wetlands to protect the shoreline from hurricanes and other storms, more low-lying areas are lost to the destructive effects of erosion.

The loss of Louisiana's wetlands is also a major blow to the fish and shellfish that use them as breeding grounds. Nearly 75 percent of all commercial marine species, including menhaden and shrimp, rely on coastal marshes and estuaries to sustain part of their life cycle. Since Louisiana's economy is largely dependent on commercial fisheries, the loss of its wetlands could cripple the state's economy, which currently draws nearly $170 million from the sea.

(opposite page)
Sediment in the Mississippi River is one of the greatest causes of wetlands loss.

The problems of Louisiana's wetlands haven't gone unnoticed. Early in 1989, a report entitled the "Louisiana Comprehensive Wetland Study" was completed by the Army Corps of Engineers. The study concluded that immediate action is needed to help save the state's most valuable resources. The study suggested a joint state/federal cost-sharing plan to help stem wetlands' loss. Without such action, Louisiana's wetlands don't stand much of a chance for survival.

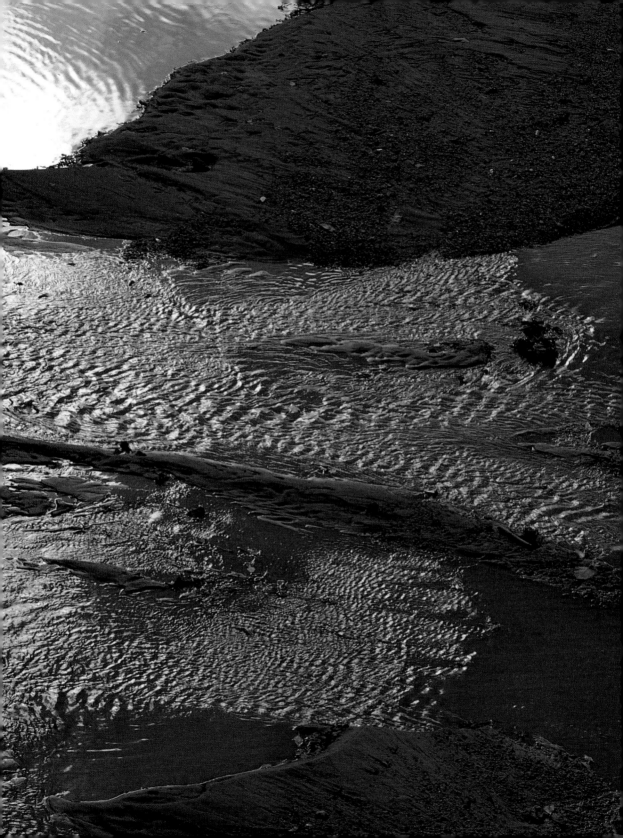

CHANGES IN THE GULF

Commercial fishing, once the backbone of the South Central coastal region, is suffering the effects of water pollution.

The Gulf of Mexico also plays an important role in the environmental and economic health of four South Central states—Texas, Louisiana, Mississippi, and Alabama. One of America's most important saltwater resources, the Gulf provides 40 percent of all U. S. commercial fish yields, 75 percent of all critical habitat for migratory waterfowl, and drainage for 66 percent of all U. S. fresh-water rivers. It generates nearly 2.5 billion pounds of commercial fish and shellfish each year.

The Gulf also supplies most of the nation's offshore gas. Substantial supplies of natural gas remain in the outer continental shelf. Nearly half of all American exports and imports pass through Gulf ports, and one sixth of the nation's population now lives in states bordering the Gulf.

Although the Gulf of Mexico plays host to large populations of wildlife such as waterfowl, shorebirds, and nesting seabirds, it also functions as a giant dump. Recent population booms have caused an extensive loss of wildlife habitat. Its waters have been over-enriched from agricultural runoff, resulting in oxygen depletion. They have also been contaminated by pesticides and toxic chemicals. Many shellfish beds have been destroyed.

Although the discharge from wastewater treatment plants and industrial sources is significant, nearly ten times more nutrients, such as agricultural fertilizers, come from sources upstream. These nutrients lead to an overabundance of microscopic plant life that eventually dies and settles to the Gulf floor, where it depletes the supply of dissolved oxygen in the water. When enough oxygen is lost, various marine organisms begin to die.

Many estuaries feeding the Gulf, including Mobile Bay, Galveston Bay, and Corpus Christi Bay, are also showing signs of oxygen depletion. In addition, nitrogen concentrations in the Mississippi River have increased twofold in recent years, probably as a result of fertilizer runoff from the nation's farm belt.

GULF TARGET AREAS

Since August 1988, the EPA has been working to develop an overall strategy designed to balance the needs of humans with those of a threatened environment. During the first year of the agency's Gulf program, the EPA drafted a five-year plan and established a network of committees whose goal is to improve the overall quality of the Gulf environment. The EPA plan points out several problem areas:

Beaches. Because of the Gulf's complex currents, waste discarded by oil rigs or ships at sea often ends up on the area's beaches. Gulf beaches more than any other in the nation are littered by Styrofoam cups, plastic bags, oil drums, and other marine debris. In September 1987 and again the following year, 15,000 volunteers removed approximately 500 tons of waste from the beaches of the four South Central Gulf states and Florida. One beach in particular—the Padre Island National Seashore—contained so many rusty oil drums that it's now on the EPA's Superfund National Priority List for emergency cleanup.

Wetlands. The EPA is working closely with the state of Louisiana to save that area's wetlands. In addition, the agency is concerned that rising temperatures from the greenhouse effect could totally destroy the wetlands of Louisiana and the rest of the Gulf.

Estuaries. The Gulf of Mexico is home to 30 important estuaries, two of which—Galveston Bay in Texas and Sarasota Bay in Florida—are the target of special restoration efforts. Both bays were recently named as part of the EPA's National Estuary Program.

OFFSHORE OIL

Another serious source of water pollution in the Gulf is offshore oil. As oil used for energy has become harder to find, oil companies have begun turning to new drilling sites, including a number of offshore sites located in the western Gulf. The results are disturbing.

Tar balls have been washing up on Texas beaches since the days of the Karankawa Indians, who collected them to use for waterproofing their woven baskets and pottery. But today, the tar is so thick in some places that it's impossible to walk across the sands without getting black feet.

For years, local beachcombers have viewed tar balls as the price they had to pay for living on the ocean—a naturally occurring nuisance like jellyfish and sea urchins. But most tar balls have been shown to be anything but natural.

Some tar balls, which are composed of thick concentrations of hydrocarbons balled together with sand, shells, and other miscellaneous debris, come from natural leaks along the continental shelf, which runs 40 to 100 miles off the Texas coast. Most, though, originate with the spills that occur when crude oil is transferred from one tanker to another before being brought to port or with such offshore oil-rig accidents as the infamous *Ixtoc I* spill in 1979.

The *Ixtoc I*, owned by SEDCO, a drilling company founded by former Texas governor Bill Clements, produced a 100-mile-long, 10-mile-wide layer of oil that began in the Bay of Campeche off the Mexican coast and slithered north across the Gulf to blacken nearly 175 miles of Texas beaches. Much of the debris ended up in sandbars off the coast, where chunks continue to be dislodged by rough seas and washed ashore.

Oil leaks and spills are damaging to the environment anywhere in the world. But they're particularly harmful in the Gulf of Mexico because of the sea's semi-closed shape. Rather like a giant baseball mitt, it tends to trap pollutants in its heel. Texas bears the brunt of the problem. Two currents, one carrying oil and other pollutants southwesterly from around Louisiana and the other northeasterly from Mexico, converge just north of Corpus Christi near Port Aransas. At this spot, there is a 10-mile stretch of sand and shells on which several tons of tar are estimated to lie, much of it from *Ixtoc I*.

CHAPTER FOUR

A TIME FOR ACTION

In the time between when you woke up this morning and when you'll eat breakfast tomorrow, another animal species will disappear from the face of the Earth. Destroyed by human carelessness, ignorance, poaching, unsound management practices, loss of habitat, or pollution, each day another animal species joins the list of tens of thousands of extinctions since the coming of people.

Seventy-eight animals were on the U.S. Department of the Interior's first list of endangered animal species in 1967. Today, more than 1,200 species round out the list. Unless we act quickly, most of these animals could soon become extinct.

The endangered animals in the South Central states include the American alligator, gray bat, Florida panther, southern bald eagle, Bachman's warbler, red-cockaded woodpecker, red wolf, American ivory-billed woodpecker, Mississippi sandhill crane, snail darter, whooping crane, Eskimo curlew, fountain darter, Mexican duck, black-footed ferret, prairie chicken, brown pelican, margay, ocelot, Texas blind salamander, Houston toad, gray wolf, Mexican wolf, jaguar, and many, many more.

(opposite page)
The ocelot, which once roamed throughout the South Central region, is today an endangered species.

Yet progress is being made toward cleaning up the environment and saving its threatened wildlife.

TURTLES STAGE A COMEBACK

As wildlife continues to disappear from the South Central United States, people are beginning to act. Since 1977, the U.S. Fish and Wildlife Service has supplied workers, vehicles, and other assistance to a Mexican program set up to aid biologists

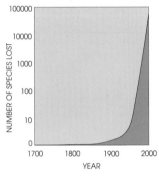

Estimated Annual Rate of Species Loss, 1700-2000

Source: Based on estimates in Norman
Myers (ed., *Gaia: An Atlas of Planet
Management* (Garden City, NY:
Anchor Books, 1984), p. 155

(opposite page)
*Drilling for offshore oil
is a major industry
near Port Aransas,
Texas, but at what cost
to the environment?*

who gather the eggs from nesting Kemp's ridley turtles. These turtles are dangerously close to extinction due to contamination of their breeding grounds by oil spills and commercial development. In exchange, the Mexican government is given about 2 percent of the annual egg production.

These eggs incubate not on Mexican beaches but in sand on Texas' Padre Island National Seashore. The eggs are flown 250 miles to Padre Island, where they hatch. The young turtles are then released to crawl down to the water. Biologists hope that the turtles "imprint" on the beach, forming a lasting impression so that they will return to it to breed once they mature.

Before the turtles reach the water, they're quickly gathered up and kept in a laboratory for a year. As soon as they're large enough to escape most natural predators, biologists return them to Padre Island where they're released back into the Gulf of Mexico.

NATURAL ORGANISMS THAT EAT OIL

Tar balls, oil slicks, and floating slime aren't exactly things the Gulf of Mexico needs more of. Yet certain ecological communities of mussels, clams, and tubeworms seem to thrive on such things, according to recent research conducted by scientists at Texas A & M University. The scientists say that natural petroleum seepage into the Gulf is occurring at several underwater sites where these recently identified colonies of sea life are thriving.

"Instead of hindering the population of organisms on the seafloor," reports Mahlon C. Kennicutt II of the university's Geochemical and Environmental Research group, "it appears that the oil seepage actually enhances it."

For decades, scientists have suspected that the natural seepage of petroleum in the Gulf means that there are significant oil reserves there for the taking. Recently, Kennicutt and his colleagues were able to observe firsthand the seepage from deep beneath the surface of the Gulf into its waters. The researchers used submarines to trace the movement of petroleum from deep within oil reservoirs in the seafloor and, in the process, discovered large mounds of oil coming out of the ground on the continental shelf off the Louisiana coast.

"It's the chemical environment created by this seepage of oil, as well as of gas, that makes the specialized communities of hydrocarbon-eating marine animals viable," according to Kennicutt.

The fact that natural sources of oil pollution have been identified along with the ecosystems that thrive on them could have a major effect on the future of offshore oil development. Future research may lead to the development of a "super-race" of marine species able to consume as much oil as we accidentally spill into marine environments. Given both time and opportunity, nature may once again find a way of protecting its own.

PUTTING WASTE TO WORK

In Austin, Texas, two city departments recently learned the value of working together to rid the city of one of its largest disposal problems—sludge from its waste-treatment plants.

Austin's Auditorium Shores Park is a popular gathering spot for the city's residents. During spring and summer, numerous festivals and outdoor concerts take place in the park. Each summer, AquaFest, with its ten nights of music and dancing, draws tens of thousands of people. In the past, Austin's City Parks and Recreation Department has had a tough time keeping the park's lawn alive, let alone green.

Then the city began experimenting with turning Austin's sludge into a beneficial slow-release fertilizer. Municipal sludge often has a high heavy metal content that prohibits its use near people. But Austin recently enacted a successful sludge pre-treatment program that limits the metals and other chemicals that are allowed to be discharged by businesses and industries into the city's sewer system. This makes Austin's sludge a perfect candidate for the newly created Dillo Dirt (named after the armadillo that's fond of rooting around in Texas gardens).

The city's Water and Wastewater Utility Department begins processing the sludge by "cooking" it. This removes most of the wastewater. The sludge is then air-dried in open concrete basins, where it's turned on a regular basis to hasten drying. Once the sludge has achieved a high enough density, various dry bulking substances are added—usually wood chips from the city's tree-trimming programs.

The entire mixture of sludge and bulking material is formed into piles and arranged in rows. The temperature of each row is monitored daily to make sure that enough heat is generated as the material composts, destroying any remaining harmful bacteria. After screening out larger wood chips, the compost is ready for use.

The Parks and Recreation staff first applied the sludge to a local soccer field at the end of the season. Within two weeks, the grass had become noticeably greener and healthier looking. And the public, which had been skeptical about the new Dillo Dirt, was impressed. Newspaper reporters for the sports section of the city's largest daily, the *American-Statesman*, as well as the University of Texas' *Daily Texan*, praised the city's work.

Then the staff spread Dillo Dirt over Auditorium Park. Once again, the results were impressive.

"We're really pleased with Dillo Dirt," says Jim Rodgers, program manager for Metropolitan Parks. "You can really tell the difference at Auditorium Shores where it was and wasn't applied…. We could take all they [the Water and Wastewater Utility] make for our baseball fields and other park areas."

Why use reprocessed sludge instead of commercially available fertilizers? According to Rodgers, "It's cheap, it's organic, it's got some nitrogen, and, frankly, when the Water and Wastewater Utility staff said they would deliver and spread it, that did the trick!"

Dillo Dirt provides an effective organic fertilizer for parklands. The recycling effort saves the city of Austin from having to landfill nearly 50 dry tons of treated sludge a day. Both are results worth cheering about.

ACTIVISM PAYS OFF

Black activist Pat Bryant founded the Gulf Coast Tenants Leadership Development Project in 1982. The project was founded in response to Reagan administration cuts in public housing and various poverty programs to help pay for a military buildup. Conducting a "Housing—Not Bombs" campaign among the poor of southern Alabama, Louisiana, and Mississippi, Bryant's group trained local leaders to mobilize their neighbors to demand social justice and better living conditions.

Soon, Bryant turned his attention to another problem facing the poor residents of "Cancer Alley." This is the lower Mississippi's toxic wasteland where one fourth of America's chemicals are produced.

"These people were miserable," according to Bryant, "because they found their lives sandwiched in between the Union Carbide and Monsanto [two large chemical companies] complexes. Their children were constantly having eye and respiratory problems."

Bryant understood that helping the poor meant more than marching for racial justice, jobs, and housing. It also meant demanding clean air and water.

Soon he and other activists learned everything they could about chemicals and how to get environmental data from the government. In early 1988, the group attended the Southern Environmental Assembly in Atlanta. Within a year, a coalition had formed linking Bryant's project with members of the Sierra Club, the Louisiana Environmental Action Network, and the Oil, Chemical, and Atomic Workers Union.

"We must put aside the foolish customs that divide us and work together, at least for the sake of our children," Bryant said as the activists launched the Great Louisiana Toxics March. For ten days, protesters demonstrated throughout "Cancer Alley," demanding reductions in the toxic emissions of local chemical companies.

After that, Bryant was named acting director of the Louisiana Toxics Project. In 1989, the Louisiana state legislature passed its first air-quality law.

"The environment is the number one problem in this country," according to Bryant. "As an African-American, my hopes and aspirations to be free are greatly dimmed by the prospect of environmental destruction. If we're going to make great strides on this problem, we're going to have to build African-American/European-American coalitions. If we can do that in the context of the environment, it will be empowering for everyone."[1]

SLOW, STEADY PROGRESS

Slowly but steadily, we're seeing a growing sense of concern over the condition of our environment. America is placing a new emphasis on the study and review of environmental issues. In the process, our natural environment—plagued by wastes, poisons, abuse, and greed—may have received a temporary reprieve.

Yet healing the wounds we've made in the environment is a difficult, time-consuming job that requires painstaking, diligent effort. It's no longer up to only a handful of concerned politicians and environmentalists. It's up to everyone.

The very technologies that have raised the standard of living for millions of people over the last hundred years have contributed to the environment's demise. We must now begin to rebuild to have a healthy, vibrant environmental community—not only for wildlife, but for us all. Only through global cooperation can we ensure that the world of tomorrow will be even more prosperous than the world of today.

WHAT WE CAN DO

At times, the issues of pollution and a healthy environment seem overwhelming. Yet there are many things individuals and groups can do to help save the environment from destruction. In the South Central United States, where stopping coastal pollution and wetlands destruction is critical to a healthy environment, citizens can join local groups or national organizations with programs on ocean and coastal issues. They can learn about current priorities, legislation, and projects related to coastal and wetlands issues. They can persuade other organizations to make marine issues their priority.

To find out more about ocean and coastal issues, consult those organizations listed later in this book. Meanwhile, here are some other things you can do.

FOR THE LAND

- Join local groups or national organizations working to save the South Central region's forests.

- Encourage the local media to devote more attention to the destruction of South Central forests. Suggest that environmental writers examine the effects of forest destruction.

(opposite page)
Recycling is one of the simplest and most effective means of reducing pollution.

- Organize a group to create a festive "Save Our Forests" day with speeches, music, games, and theatrical presentations all geared to creating a greater awareness of the importance of the region's forests to a healthy environment.

- Help organize a town meeting in your community and invite congressional representatives, civic leaders, and conservation groups to discuss forest-related issues.

- Encourage local schools, colleges, and libraries to obtain and present information on deforestation and its effects on the area's environment.

- Offer to help a local library put together an exhibit on local forests.

- Recycle cans, bottles, paper, and plastic in order to save our natural resources and reduce solid waste.

- Avoid the use of toxic or hazardous chemicals around the house—including those hidden in everyday household products such as cleansers.

FOR THE WATER

- Write to the National Oceanic and Atmospheric Administration and ask them to speed up their designation of national marine sanctuaries.

- Support efforts to protect those remaining undeveloped coastlines from future development.

- Encourage plans to set up marine reserves—places where future development is restricted or prohibited.

- Work for the stricter regulation of solid-waste disposal and more efficient alternative uses for these wastes, using the city of Austin as one example of success in the area.

- Attend meetings concerned with such coastal issues as waste disposal in the ocean; the building of new industrial and power plants; wetlands protection; oil, gas, and mineral reserve development; and the prevention and cleanup of accidental oil spills and discharges.

- Conserve water use in your home and on your property.

- Avoid using chemical fertilizers and weed killers.

FOR THE AIR

- Find out about major sources of air pollution in your area—whether they're motor vehicles, power plants, industrial operations, or municipal waste incinerators.

- Learn whether or not your state's air-quality standards are in compliance with federal regulations.

- Write to your local government representatives asking for limits on chlorofluorocarbons (CFCs), a major contributor to the greenhouse effect, in home insulation, household and automobile coolants, and fire extinguishers.

- Support a statewide ban on vehicles with air conditioners containing CFCs; the state of Vermont has already enacted such legislation effective as of 1992.

- Write to local representatives about strengthening the Clean Air Act to improve air quality and limit damage from pollutants.

- Ask local representatives to create a commission to consider statewide actions limiting greenhouse gas emissions, as the state of Missouri recently did.

- Plant as many trees around your town as possible. Trees help conserve energy by shading buildings in the summer, and they absorb carbon dioxide, a leading contributor to the greenhouse effect.

- Save electricity by turning off unnecessary lights and appliances and turning down the air conditioner in summer. Use ceiling fans and install storm windows and insulation to reduce energy consumption.

- Volunteer for service in organizations active in preventing air pollution and in monitoring and enforcing air-quality standards.

- Join organizations and subscribe to newsletters to keep you up to date on the latest developments in clean-air legislation.

- Write letters to the editors of local newspapers on the subject of air pollution.

- Find out whether your school has a course or program relating to the greenhouse effect. If not, suggest that it start one.

The following toll-free hot-line telephone numbers provide information ranging from pesticide use to asbestos in homes; from hazardous-waste disposal to chemical-emergency preparedness.

- Asbestos Hotline (1-800-334-8571). Provides information on asbestos and asbestos abatement programs; Mon. to Fri., 8:15 a.m. to 5 p.m.

- Chemical Emergency Preparedness Program Hotline (1-800-535-0202). For information on community preparedness for chemical accidents, etc.; Mon. to Fri., 8:30 a.m. to 4:30 p.m.

- Inspector General's Whistle Blower Hotline (1-800-424-4000). For confidential reporting of EPA-related waste, fraud, abuse, or mismanagement; Mon. to Fri., 10 a.m. to 3 p.m.

- National Pesticides Telecommunications Network Hotline (1-800-858-7378). Provides information about pesticides, toxicity, management, health and environmental effects, safety practices, and cleanup and disposal; 7 days, 24 hours a day.

- National Response Center Hotline (1-800-424-8802). For reporting oil and hazardous chemical spills; 7 days, 24 hours a day.

- Superfund Hotline (1-800-424-9346). Provides Superfund information and technical assistance; Mon. to Fri., 8:30 a.m to 4:30 p.m.

The following list includes organizations that can provide information and materials on various topics of environmental concern in the South Central states.

American Rivers
Conservation Council
801 Pennsylvania
Ave. SE
Washington, D.C. 20003
202-547-6900

American Water
Resources Association
5410 Grosvenor Lane
Bethesda, MD 20814
301-492-8600

Center for Clean
Air Policy
444 N. Capitol St.
Washington, D.C. 20001
202-624-7709

Center for Marine
Conservation
1725 DeSales St. NW
Washington, D.C. 20036
202-429-5609

Citizen's Clearinghouse
for Hazardous Wastes
P.O. Box 926
Arlington, VA 22216
703-276-7070

Citizens for Ocean Law
1601 Connecticut
Ave. NW
Washington, D.C. 20009
202-462-3737

Coastal Programs
Division Bureau of
Marine Resources
P.O. Box 959
Long Beach, MS 39560
601-864-4602

Coastal Resources
Division
Dept. of Natural
Resources
P.O. Box 44396
Capitol Station
Baton Rouge, LA 70804
504-342-4500

Common Cause
2030 M St. NW
Washington, D.C. 20036
202-833-1200

Council for Solid Waste
Solutions
1275 K St. NW
Washington, D.C. 20005
202-371-5319

Council on
Environmental Quality
722 Jackson Place NW
Washington, D.C. 20006
202-395-5750

Defenders of Wildlife
1244 19th St. NW
Washington, D.C. 20036
202-659-9510

Department of
Conservation and
Natural Resources
64 N. Union St.
Montgomery, AL 36193
205-261-3346

Department of
Environmental
Management
1751 Federal Dr.
Montgomery, AL 36130
205-271-7700

Department of Natural
Resources
Bureau of Pollution
Control
P.O. Box 10385
Jackson, MS 39209
601-961-5171

Environmental Action
1525 New Hampshire
Ave. NW
Washington, D.C. 20036
202-745-4870

Environmental Action
1525 New Hampshire
Ave. NW
Washington, D.C. 20036
202-745-4870

Environmental Coalition
for North America
1325 G St. NW
Washington, D.C. 20005
202-289-5009

Environmental
Defense Fund
275 Park Ave. S.
New York, NY 10010
212-505-2100

Friends of the Earth
530 7th St. SE
Washington, D.C. 20003
202-543-4312

Greenpeace USA
1436 U St. NW
Washington, D.C. 20009
202-462-1177

Izaak Walton League
1701 N. Ft. Myer Dr.
Arlington, VA 22209
703-528-1818

Keep America
Beautiful, Inc.
Mill River Plaza
9 W. Broad St.
Stamford, CT 06902
(Phone # unavailable)

National Association for
Plastic Container
Recovery
5024 Parkway Plaza
Blvd.
Charlotte, NC 28217
704-357-3250

National Audubon
Society
833 Third Ave.
New York, NY 10022
212-832-3200

National Clean Air
Coalition
801 Pennsylvania Ave.
SE
Washington, D.C. 20003
202-543-8200

National Coalition
against the Misuse of
Pesticide
530 7th St. SE
Washington, D.C. 20001
202-543-5450

National Coalition for
Marine Conservation
1 Post Office Square
Boston, MA 02109
617-338-2909

National Geographic
Society
17th and M Streets NW
Washington, D.C. 20036
202-857-7000

National Recycling
Coalition
45 Rockefeller Plaza,
Room 2350
New York, NY 10111
212-765-1800

National Wildlife
Federation
1412 16th St. NW
Washington, D.C. 20036
202-737-2024

The Nature Conservancy
1815 N. Lynn St.
Arlington, VA 22209
703-841-4860

The Oceanic Society
1536 16th St. NW
Washington, D.C. 20036
(Phone # unavailable)

Sierra Club
530 Bush St.
San Francisco, CA 94108
415-981-8634

Soil and Water
Conservation Society
7515 Northeast
Ankeny Rd.
Ankeny, IA 50021-9764
(Phone # unavailable)

Texas Committee on
Natural Resources
4144 Cochran Chapel
Rd.
Dallas, TX 75209
214-352-8370

United Nations
Environment Program
2 U.N. Plaza
New York, NY 10022
212-963-8139

U.S. Dept. of Agriculture
Independence Ave.
between 12th and 14th
Streets SW
Washington, D.C. 20250
202-477-8732

U.S. Environmental
Protection Agency
401 M St. SW
Washington, D.C. 20460
202-541-4040

U.S. Fish and Wildlife
Service
Dept. of the Interior
Washington, D.C. 20240
202-343-1100

U.S. Forest Service
P.O. Box 96090
Washington, D.C. 20090
202-447-3957

Water Commission
P.O. Box 13087
Capitol Station
Austin, TX 78711
512-463-8028

Wilderness Society
1400 Eye St. NW
Washington, D.C. 20005
202-842-3400

Worldwatch Institute
1776 Massachusetts Ave.
NW
Washington, D.C. 20036
202-452-1999

World Wildlife Fund
1250 24th St. NW
Washington, D.C. 20037
202-293-4800

N O T E S

CHAPTER ONE: THE LAND WE WALK

1. *As We Live and Breathe*, National Geographic Society, 1971, p. 13.
2. *The Global Ecology Handbook* (Boston: Beacon Press, 1990), p. 84.
3. David Rains Wallace, *Life in the Balance* (New York: Harcourt Brace Jovanovich, 1987), p. 46.
4. Susan McCarthy, "Preserve Protectors Take Heart," *Sierra*, November/December, 1989, pp. 91 - 92.
5. *The Global Ecology Handbook*, p. 248.
6. Ibid, p. 248, figure 13.2.
7. Ruth Caplan, *Our Earth, Ourselves* (New York: Bantam Books, 1990), p. 116.

CHAPTER TWO: THE AIR WE BREATHE

1. *The Global Ecology Handbook*, p. 221.
2. Jon Naar, *Design for a Livable Planet* (New York: Harper & Row, 1990), pp. 79 - 80.
3. Caplan, *Our Earth, Ourselves*, p. 90.
4. Ibid, pp. 88 - 90.
5. *The Universal Almanac 90* (Kansas City, MO: Universal Press Syndicate Company, 1989), pp. 370 - 371.
6. *The Global Ecology Handbook*, p. 232.
7. Ibid, p. 231.
8. Caplan, *Our Earth, Ourselves*, p. 24.
9. Ibid, p. 23.
10. *The Global Ecology Handbook*, p. 233.
11. *The Washington Post*, March 21, 1989, p. A17.

CHAPTER THREE: THE WATER WE DRINK

1. *The Universal Almanac 90*, p. 372.
2. Ibid, p. 372.
3. Wallace, *Life in the Balance*, p. 227.
4. Ibid, p. 227.

CHAPTER FOUR: A TIME FOR ACTION

1. Caplan, *Our Earth, Ourselves*, pp. 140 - 141.

Aquatic. Of or relating to life in the water.

Air pollution. The transfer of contaminating substances into the atmosphere, usually as a result of human activities.

Algae. Primitive green plants, many of which are microscopic.

Aquifer. Water-bearing rock or soil.

Atmosphere. A mass of gases surrounding the Earth.

Biological control. The use of a pest's natural predators and parasites to control its population.

Biome. A specific type of environment capable of supporting life.

Biosphere. That part of the Earth, including its atmosphere, in which life can exist.

Carcinogen. A substance known to cause cancer.

Carnivore. A flesh-eating animal.

Clear-cutting. The practice of cutting all trees and shrubs from the land.

Dust. Tiny particulate materials that are primarily the product of wind erosion of soil.

Ecology. The branch of science concerned with the interrelationship of organisms and their environment.

Ecosystem. A functioning unit of the environment that includes all living organisms and physical features within a given area.

Energy. The ability to perform work.

Erosion. The removal and transportation of soil by wind, running water, or glaciation.

Estuary. A coastal ecosystem where fresh water and salt water meet.

Extinction. The disappearance of a species from Earth.

Fertilizer. A substance used to make soil more productive.

Food chain. A sequence of organisms in which each member feeds on the member below it, such as an owl, rabbit, and grass.

Fossil fuels. Various fuel materials such as coal, oil, and natural gas created from the remains of once-living organisms.

Greenhouse effect. The increase in solar-radiated infrared light waves in the Earth's atmosphere; the increase is caused by an accumulation of such gases as methane, nitrogen oxides, ozone, and chlorofluorocarbons (CFCs).

Groundwater. Water that is contained in sub-surface rock and soil formations.

Hazardous waste. The extremely dangerous by-product of civilization that, by its chemical makeup, is harmful to life.

Heavy metal. A metal such as mercury or lead that is harmful to life.

Herbicide. A chemical compound used to kill plants.

Herbivore. A plant-eating animal.

Irrigation. The process of diverting water from its source to farmland in order to increase crop yields.

Landfill. A site for the disposal of garbage and other waste products.

Leaching. The dissolving and transporting of materials by water seeping downward through soil.

Levee. An embankment or dike to prevent flooding.

Logging. The cutting of trees for lumber or for the purpose of clearing land.

Marsh. A parcel of soft, wet land.

Mineral. A solid material characterized by an orderly internal arrangement of atoms and a fixed chemical composition.

Nuclear waste. The long-lived, extremely dangerous by-product of nuclear energy or nuclear weapons production.

Organic farming. The process of farming without the use of environmentally dangerous chemicals in the form of fertilizers or pesticides.

Particulates. Extremely small bits of dust, soot, soil, etc., that may become airborne.

Pesticide. A general term for any of a large number of chemical compounds used to kill pests such as insects, weeds, fungi, bacteria, etc.

Poaching. The act of taking game or fish illegally.

Pollution. A general term for environmental contaminants.

Recycling. The recovery and reuse of material resources.

Rock. A stonelike material usually composed of a combination of minerals.

Runoff. Water that moves across the surface of the land faster than the soil can absorb it.

Salinization. The increase of salt in soil or water.

Smog. A visible mixture of solid, liquid, and gaseous air pollutants that are harmful both to human beings and to the environment.

Soil. A living system of weathered rock, organic matter, air, and water in which plants grow.

Superfund. A federal government fund created for the emergency cleanup of the United States' most environmentally hazardous waste sites.
submerged beneath water.

Tar ball. An accumulation of hardened oil, sand, shells, and other debris as a result of oil spills or naturally seeping oil from the bed of the ocean.

Toxic waste. The extremely dangerous by-product of chemical production or use.

Water pollution. The transfer of contaminating substances into water, usually as a result of human activities.

Water table. The highest level of a groundwater reservoir.

Wetlands. Land containing a high moisture content.

"Abundance of New Life Forms Found Deep within Earth." *National Wildlife*, October/November 1988, p. 29.

Budiansky, Stephen, and Robert F. Black. "Tons and Tons of Trash and No Place To Put It." *U.S. News and World Report*, Dec. 14, 1987, pp. 58-62.

Carothers, Andre. "Living Next to the Landfill." *Greenpeace*, July/September 1987, p. 11.

Carothers, Andre. "The Death of Ellenton." *Greenpeace*, May/June 1988, p. 13.

Council of State Governments. *The Book of States.* Lexington, Kentucky, 1988.

"Drought and Wetlands Drainage Take a Heavy Toll on Many Species." *National Wildlife*, February/March 1989, p. 34.

Earth Report ,The. Los Angeles: Price Stern Sloan, Inc., 1988.
Grossman, Karl. *The Poison Conspiracy.* Sag Harbor, New York: The Permanent Press, 1983.

Jubera, Drew. "Texas Primer: The Tar Ball." *Texas Monthly*, August 1987, p. 102.

Lewis, Jack. "Changing the Fate of the Gulf." *EPA Journal*, September/October 1989, p. 46.

Lowrey, Leon. "Mishap & Mayhem at Bomb Plants." *Environmental Action*, November/December 1988, p. 8.

McReynolds, Maureen. "Putting Sludge to Work." *EPA Journal*, November/December 1989, p. 21.

Moran, Joseph M.; Michael D. Morgan, and James H. Wiersma. *An Introduction to Environmental Sciences.* Boston: Little, Brown and Company, 1973.

National Geographic Society. *As We Live and Breathe.* Washington, D.C., 1971.

Peterson, Cass. "Scenic Sites under Siege." *National Wildlife*, June/July 1987, p. 44.

"Record Ozone Levels and an Acid Rain Stalemate Obscure Progress." *National Wildlife*, February/March 1989, p. 35.

Rooney, Peggy. "Louisiana's Wetlands Calamity." *EPA Journal*, September/October 1989, p. 37.

Stiak, Jim. "When Toxics Reduce Recycling." *Environmental Action*, May/June 1987, p. 9.

Wagner, Richard H. *Environment and Man*. New York: W. W. Norton & Co., Inc., 1974.

Wallace, David Rains. *Life in the Balance*. Orlando, FL: Harcourt Brace Jovanovich, 1987.

Worldwatch Institute. *State of the World*. New York: W. W. Norton & Co., Inc., 1981.

I N D E X

Alabama 7, 25, 30, 38, 48
Alligators 8, 11, 12, 43
Aquifers 16
Arkansas 7, 15, 27 30,
Armadillos 8, 20, 46
Army Corps of Engineers 34
Austin 46 - 47, 52

Bachman's warbler 43
Bacteria 8, 47
Bald cypress 11, 20
Bass, largemouth 8
Bay of Campeche 41
Bayous 8, 12
Beaches 39 - 41, 44
Bears 20
Bentsen, Lloyd 21
Big Sandy 20
Big Thicket National Preserve 19
Biomes 8
Black-footed ferret 43
Bluebirds 8
Brown pelican 43
Bryant, Pat 47 - 48

Cancer 17, 25
Cancer Alley 26, 48
Carbon monoxide 25 - 27
Carcinogen polyvinyl chloride
  [PVC] 21
Chlorofluorocarbons [CFCs] 31, 53
Clements, Bill 41
Coal 26, 32
Commercial fisheries 36
Continental shelf 36, 40, 44
Corpus Christi 41
Corpus Christi Bay 39
Council on Economic Priorities 22 - 23
Crocodiles 11

DDT 17
Department of Commerce and
  Congressional Budget Office 23
Dillo Dirt 46 - 47

Dioxin 23
Drynan, Dr. John 18
Dioxin 23
Drynan, Dr. John 18
Dust Bowl 15

Egrets 20
Endrin 17 - 18
Environmental Protection Agency
  [EPA] 17 - 18, 23, 26, 30, 33, 39, 40
Erosion 35 - 36
Eskimo curlew 43

Fertilizer 18, 21, 39, 46, 47
Florida panther 43
Food chain 12, 18, 35
Fossil fuel 27, 32, 33

Galveston Bay 39, 40
Garcia, Hector 20
Global warming 32
Gray bat 43
Gray wolf 43
Greenhouse effect 31, 32, 33, 40
Gulf Coast Tenants Leadership
  Development Project 47 - 48
Gulf of Mexico 7, 35, 36, 38, 40, 41, 44

Hazardous-waste disposal 23
Hazardous-waste sites 23
Heavy metals 21, 27, 35, 46
Hydrocarbons 25, 26, 27, 40, 46

Integrated pest management [IPM] 18
Irrigation 16
Ivory-billed woodpecker 19, 20, 43
Ixtoc I 41

Jaguar 43

Kansas 7, 8, 15, 18
Kemp's ridley turtles 44
Kennicutt II, Mahlon C. 44
Kentucky 7, 27

Landfills 21, 30, 33, 35, 47
Lead 25, 27
Logging 18 - 21
Lost Heart 18 - 21
Louisiana 7, 12, 20 - 23, 30, 35 - 38,
  40 - 41, 44, 48
"Louisiana Comprehensive Wetland
  Study" 36
Louisiana Environmental Action
Network 48
Louisiana Territory 7 - 8
Louisiana Toxics Project 48
Love Canal 30

Mangroves 11
Mannchen, Brand 20
Margay 43
Marshlands 12, 36
Methane 25, 31, 33
Mexican duck 43
Mexican wolf 43
Mississippi 7, 30, 38, 48
Mississippi River 7, 17, 21, 30, 36, 39, 48
Mississippi sandhill crane 43
Missouri 7, 8, 15, 16, 23, 30
Mobile Bay 39
Monsanto 48
Mountain lions 19

National Resources Defense Council 30
Nitrogen oxides 25, 26, 31

Ocelot 43
Offshore gas 39
Offshore oil 40 - 41
Ogallala aquifer 16
Oil 23, 32, 35, 39 - 41, 44 - 46
Oil spills 35, 44 - 46
Oil, Chemical, and Atomic Workers
  Union 48
Oklahoma 7, 8, 15, 16, 18
Organization for Economic Cooperation
  and Development [OECD] 26
Otters 20
Oxygen 27, 33, 39
Oxygen depletion 39
Ozone 25, 27

Padre Island National Seashore 40
Particulates 25, 26
Pesticides 17, 18, 21, 35, 39
Photochemical oxidants 27

Polyvinyl chloride [PVC] 21
Port Aransas 41
Prairie chicken 43

Red wolf 43
Red-cockaded woodpecker 19, 43

Salinization 16
SEDCO 41
Sediment 36
Sierra Club 20, 48
Smog 27
Snail darter 43
Southern bald eagle 43
Sulfur dioxide 25, 26 - 27
Swamps 11

Tar balls 40
Tennessee 7, 23, 30
Texas 7 - 8, 12, 15, 16, 19, 20, 23, 25, 30,
  38, 40 - 41, 43, 44, 46 - 47
Texas blind salamander 43
Texas Farm Bureau 20
Times Beach 23
Topsoil 15, 16
Toxic chemicals 18, 23, 26, 27, 30, 39
Toxic waste 21, 23, 30, 35, 48

U.S. Fish and Wildlife Service 43
Union Carbide 48
Urban developments 35

Velsicol Chemical Corporation 17

Wetlands 7 - 8, 11, 12, 35 - 36, 40, 51
Whooping crane 43
Wilson, Charles 20 - 21

3